MOUNDS LIGHTHOUSE

Ancient Guidance

BY

Charles Leman Burks

Published by Amz Legacy Press

Copyright © Charles Leman Burks

All rights reserved. No part of this book may be reproduced, stored in a retrieval system, or transmitted in any form or by any means—electronic, mechanical, photocopying, recording, or otherwise—without the prior written permission of the publisher, except for brief quotations used in reviews or articles.

This is a work of [fiction/non-fiction]. Any resemblance to actual persons, living or dead, events, or places is purely coincidental. The information provided in this book is for educational and informational purposes only.

For permissions, contact: burkspom@gmail.com

Dedication

To my grandparents, Harvey and Mary May Burks, who showed me the Promised Land, and to the indigenous voices of the past and present—may your stories echo forever.

Introduction: A Child of the 33rd Parallel

On a Friday, March 5, 1976, at 8:04 AM, an AB negative child was born at Conway Hospital Monroe, Louisiana, Ouachta (Washitaw) Parish to the parents of Martha Burks, birthday March 17, and Michael Harden, birthday March 10.

His name shall be Charles Leman (Lamont) Burks. Yes, my middle name was named after Lamont on Sanford and son, smiles. But Martha also gave the name to all of her favorite farm animals: chickens, cows, pigs, horses, donkeys, dogs, and cats.

Life was amazingly different on the 33rd parallel, Beauf (Buffalo) River basin. Being the only male left on the farm besides my grandfather Harvey Burks, my grandmother decided to sail the 180 acres of farmland with the help of Mary May Burks and migrated to a small town in the Bay Area, Pittsburgh, California, in which my parents and I have been traveling back-and-forth for four years.

The Promised Land is what Pawpaw Burks called P town on arrival, but after the second fall with me being in bed with them both times and battling cancer, He never regained consciousness and passed when I was the age of four.

Remembering one phenomenal transpired.

One day, while at my grandmother's house, I entered the back bathroom where Pawpaw kept his fishing poles. As I entered, I was met by a divine bright light that swept me off the floor. I was suspended in midair with my chin up, arms hanging down, and my kneecap hanging downwards.

I just want to fast-forward six years of my life to significant events happening now. At the age of seven, I fell off a 12-foot overpass. Also, within that time, my parents divorced, and within the next three years, my mother remarried, who would become Sergeant Major Justice. My dad raised me from age 7, and we now live in Oceanside, California, Camp Pendleton.

Chapter 1

The Ouachita Legacy

There was a mountain-building event between the South American plate beneath the North American plate called the Ouachita orogeny, which is approximately 360,000,000 to 312,000,000 years old and lasted 48 million years in the late Devonian into early Pennsylvania of the Paleozoic era.

The Ouachita Mountains comprise complexly folded and faulted Paleozoic-age sedimentary rocks deposited initially in mostly deep marine environments.

Reference: Arkansas River Valley and Ouachita Mountains.

"Big Hunting Grounds" is Choctaw, meaning for Ouachita; to others, it's "Silver Water." Before the Louisiana Purchase, more or less the present-day Monroe established a point of contact on the banks of the Ouachita River for the fur traders and Indians.

References: History of Ouachita Parish.

The Ouachita Mountains are known as the quartz crystals capital of the world after the Ouachita Orogeny, with crystals up to several feet in length.

References: Ouachita Mountains-Wikipedia.

In 2016, an 8,000-pound piece of natural quartz was found in an Arkansas mine and is now on display at the Smithsonian Natural History Museum.

The article goes on to state how Arkansas's Ouachita mountains are a hot pad for quartz, and that understanding the temperature, chemistry, and pressure conditions that it takes to grow these quartz crystals can help inform us about the geological context of a region at the time of Crystal formation and vice versa, said Farfan. I would like to consider Dr. Gabriela Farfan and vice versa.

References: Massive slabs of quartz crystals are in public view at the Smithsonian.

Our natural environment surrounds us, and everything in it influences our thinking, opinions, and moods. The climate influences us, and pollution can affect our health. Even human survival might be affected by natural resources.

References: How The Environment Shapes Us-Medium.

The ancients knew this and built great civilizations using the natural resources of their environment, including those of the Egyptians, Maya, Olmec, and Mound Building Ouachitas (Washitaw).

Now, imagine a river from your community environment that begins and flows from mountains, which are the world's quartz crystals.

The amount of purification took place in all the land there, from the second tallest mountain peak of the South American plate to the North American plate coming together in the Ouachita orogeny...

Not just crystals of purification, but watching our River is relevant to sustaining human livelihoods from different ecosystems, drinking water, irrigation, and industrial use, not to mention ancient times for transportation, trading, and hydroelectric power.

I and my sister at the bay Pittsburg CA

My grandfather Hearvy Burks and grandmother Marry Mays Burks

Grandmother Marry Mays Burks

My grandmother father Ed Mays

I and my mother Martha Burks Justice at Ed Mays grave

Great grandfather Ed Mays headstone born in 1875

My great Uncle Pekal Mays

Ed Mays sister my great great Auntie Sallie Mays, and Auntie Eula, and great Auntie Matha Mays

Chapter 2 Ancient Empires

In 1993, the Washitaw (Ouachita) Indigenous nation of Moundbuilders received its United Nations number 215/93 to date. As one of Henry Turner's living heirs, the Empress has recovered the title to 68,883 acres of land comprising most of the northern part of the said state of Louisiana. The Washitaw never drew boundaries. We are the original inhabitants of all the lands. From wherever you find Mound sites, you see part of the Empire.

References: empirewashitaw.com

The Louisiana territory was part of the 1803 Louisiana Purchase and lay north of the 33rd parallel.

References: 33rd Parallel North-Wikipedia.

There are many arguments that one building on this line has close links with Freemasonry, religious communities, and even secret societies, but various enigmatic places like these have historical facts attributed to them. Even the Roswell area is popular for its history of UFO-related subjects.

References: The Mystery of Parallel 33 Everything Is Connected to This Number English-News.

Many speculate extraterrestrials (UFOs) in many ancient cultural societies. The lid of the last Maya King K'inich Janaab' Pakal burial tomb sarcophagus at the ruins of Palenque Chiapas, Mexico, shows King Pakal traveling through space, his hands on the controls of a spaceship.

References: Exploring Palenque, Mayan City Lost in The Mexican Jungle-Dani Redd.

Here's one more fascinating article about the recently found Maya map. It depicts extraterrestrials interacting with the ancient Mayan civilization.

At the end of the article, it reads that regardless of the outcome of ongoing investigations, the discovery has ignited an absorbing renewed interest in exploring ancient civilizations with a fresh perspective.

References: Ancient Maya Map Found Proves That Contact Between Humans and Aliens Has Existed for A Long Time. Jan 6th 2024

Another aspect of higher power influences is the idea that we come from the divine and that this divinity lives in us.

Our limitations can be transcended with this power from what limits us, which is fear.

Artists who write music say these divine flows through them instead of coming to them.

In like manner, we have the divine flow of power to transcend our limitations by becoming our best version.

In which scientist Gregg Braden explains the bridge between science and spirituality, he finds the human DNA numbers to words that read "God Eternal Within the Body," in which some ancient text depicts our body as the temple.

References: The Spiritual Battle for Our Humanity: Transhumanism, DNA, AI, And Our Forgotten Past, Gregg Braden, Know Thyself.

Me on the Ouachita(Washitaw)River

Me and Imperial Big Chief David Montana of the Washitaw Nation (Mardi Gras Indians) next to a Mound on the Ouachita(Washitaw)River 2020 June !9th Celebration

Right to Left Imperial Big Queen Amor Amenkum, I, and Imperial Big Chief David Montana on a Mound at Ouachita (Washitaw) River

Me on Clear Lake right side of Boeuf(Buffalo)River Louisiana "Boeuf River Basin

Me in Aw, of Ancestral energy at ancient Palenque Temple of Inscriptions "K'inich Janaab' Pakal(the Great) place of burial, the oldest verivide ruler of the Americas at almost 70 years reigning, and being the fifth longest of any Monarch in history. Palenque, Chiapas, Mexica

Me viewing from Temple of the Cross, with the Palace observatory Tower in the back, left, with the Temple of the Sun in the back far right

Chapter 3: More Roots of Empires

Worlds from four months ago, I have not done intensive research on the site's geographic area or couture. I'm overwhelmed by the generosity, care, and warm family welcoming of the Danny Di Paa (Indigenous ancient gardens of Monte Albàn).

I asked: This is my first time meeting Mr. Juarez. Why did you have me to look at exhibit tumb 7 first?

Mr. Juarez answered: That's the most important thing and a piece of history of Monte Albàn; it's where they found the most significant amount of gold in Mexico's history.

Me: Wow, so let me ask you this. Besides the tomb, would you say that this whole excavation here was of my complexion first as far as the Olmec?

Mr. Juarez answered: Yes, it was a mix. People from different tribes, even from New Mexico, and people from New Mexico came from Georgia and North Carolina.

Me: Right

Mr. Juarez continues: Black communities came here, and it was a mix, even if the history doesn't show that much. But the remaining of our stuff isn't just here, even in those Southern places.

Me: Right, so the first people here were of dark complexion?

Mr. Juarez: Darker than us.

Me: Awesome.

Mr. Juarez: Darker than us.

Me: Thank YOU, I just have to document this.

Mr. Juarez: it'll be my pleasure to help you out.

Me: Thank you, likewise.

Keeping in contact with Mr. Juarez, he invited me to the house to meet his father, brother, and his brother's wife.

Mr. Juarez told me his father was the last link between the first and last Indian (indigenous) president, Benito Juarez.

Me: so, what would you like to be recognized for, Mr. Juarez?

Mr. Juarez: As a native of Mexico, a native of the surroundings of Monte Albàn, the owner of this place to take care of it and not take advantage of it.

Me: That's where the pyramids are?

Mr. Juarez: Yes, to take care of it.

Me: Awesome.

Mr. Juarez: To keep it.

Me: Yes.

Mr. Juarez: So, the whole world will know and come and enjoy our culture.

Me: Awesome.

Mr. Juarez: As I say, my dad is the last link, and he wants to be recognized as the last link of that Indian who ruled Mexico.

Me: Yes.

Mr. Juarez turns to his father and asks,

Mr. Juarez: Around what time, Papa? It was a very short time because he was persecuted by the enemy. See, he was ruling well towards the poor people; the rich people don't like him, they don't like him.

Mr. Juarez's brother responded: Even though he was the president, he was the first refugee in New Orleans, America.

Jay interprets the translation into Spanish.

Mrs. Chica stands with her father and grandchild while her mother sits with a piece of cane pole touching the earth. As a matter of fact, my mom and dad are the first generation. He's 96, and she's 88, and they raised me here as a second generation. My daughter is the third generation, and my grandchild is the fourth. All of them were raised right here at Monte Albàn.

Me asking: Do you like the conditions here at Monte Albàn?

Mrs. Chica's response: I don't like the conditions because they are humiliating, and I feel ashamed of how they treat me, but we have no choice. For this reason, we continue working here at Monte Albàn until today.

Me: Wow

Me asking: What do you wanna see happen?

Mrs. Chica's response: I would like a decent place with better intentions. I would like to dignify my names, my parents' names, and all my family's names. The conditions are not right today. Even though we have umbrellas in that band, we had permission three years ago, not before then. The umbrellas go bad because of the wind, the hell, or the rain. Even though we are still in this condition, the parking lot is a dangerous place to stay, and we would like to change that.

Me: Absolutely.

Me: You guys are a significant part of this site. Without you, there would be no tourists here, so you must be in good condition to keep up with Monte Albàn.

Me asking: Is there anything you would like the world to know about the indigenous people here?

Mrs. Chica's response: I am grateful you are here, and so the word can be spread we are here.

Me: It's an honor.

Mrs. Chica's response: Because I have no choice, I have to continue working here Because I have no other way to bring food to the table. I want the world to know that I must keep working in this condition, even if nobody hears my voice, but I want the world to know. We are reckoned alive because many accidents happened in this parking lot in the life of a being here. We used to work inside, but they'd been kicking us out gradually until we ended up in the parking lot.

On another wonderful occasion, I interviewed Mrs. G. Let's just nicely call her.

Mr. Juarez interprets Mrs., explaining how difficult times were in the past to present here at Monte Albàn.

These ancient stairs to the pyramid structures were the limit we could not cross, or we would get in trouble.

Mr. Juarez: Those steps.

Me: Oh, Wow.

Mrs. G: You can walk around and sell your stuff here, just not from the steps and up.

Me: Oh, Wow.

Mrs. G continues: Here we have a little stand with two undersized plywoods, like a little basket, and they can offer it by giving it to people in welcoming and following them; back then, they had to.

Like the guy sitting by the tree, that's one of the things that will hurt us, and they are allowed, and we are not. There is a rule that they can sell and walk all over. That's what you were trying to show the world: that they are discriminating against us. They can sell their stuff, and we cannot. And we have the same right. There are 50 in total, 50 of which sell their things in locations inside the ruins, but we cannot do that.

They sell their stuff that we sell for 10 times more than we do.

Me: Wow, Amazing.

Mr. Juarez: That's one of the things.

Me in Oaxaca Mexico

Me at Monte Albàn Tomb 7: Monte Albàn, a Zepotec city and archaeological site, is famous for it's Tomb 7, a burial site discovered in 1931 by Alfonso Caso, that holds a vast collection of artifacts, including gold, silver, turquoise, and intricate bone carvings, showcasing Zapotec and Mixtec cultures, but not directly connected to the OLMEC civilization. Although Monte Albàn and Tomb 7 are most closely associated with the

Zapotec and Mixtec cultures, the Olmec civilization was Present in the region Earlier. References: AI

Mr. Juarez and I meeting down below Monte Albàn on the Mountain

Mr. Juarez family and home down below
Monte Albàn on the Mountain

. Mrs. Chica and family (Danny Di Paa) at
Monte Albàn parking lot

Mrs. G, family, and I meeting over Bruch at Chocolate Mayordomo, Oaxaca, Mexico

Danny Di Paa on the Mountain down below Monte Albàn

Learning Ancient Arts and Crafts with Danny Di Paa on the Mountain passed on by their ancestors makes participation exercisable

Feeling right at home gathering, and cross referencing Herstory while enjoying a fresh cooked meal with beautiful people(Danny Di Paa)

Danny Di Paa and I eating at CAFÉ LOCO Santa Cruz Amilpas, Mexico

Enjoying the streets of Oaxaca City, Mexico

Drying my clothes in Santa Cruz Amilpas, Mexico

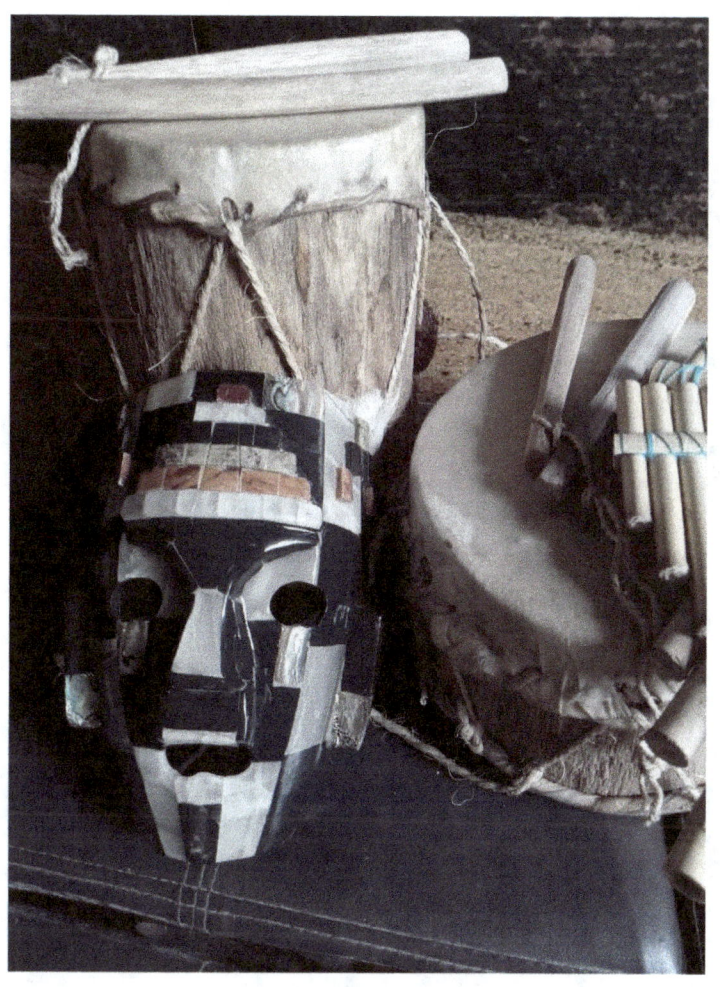

A few items I purchased on and off the Mountain

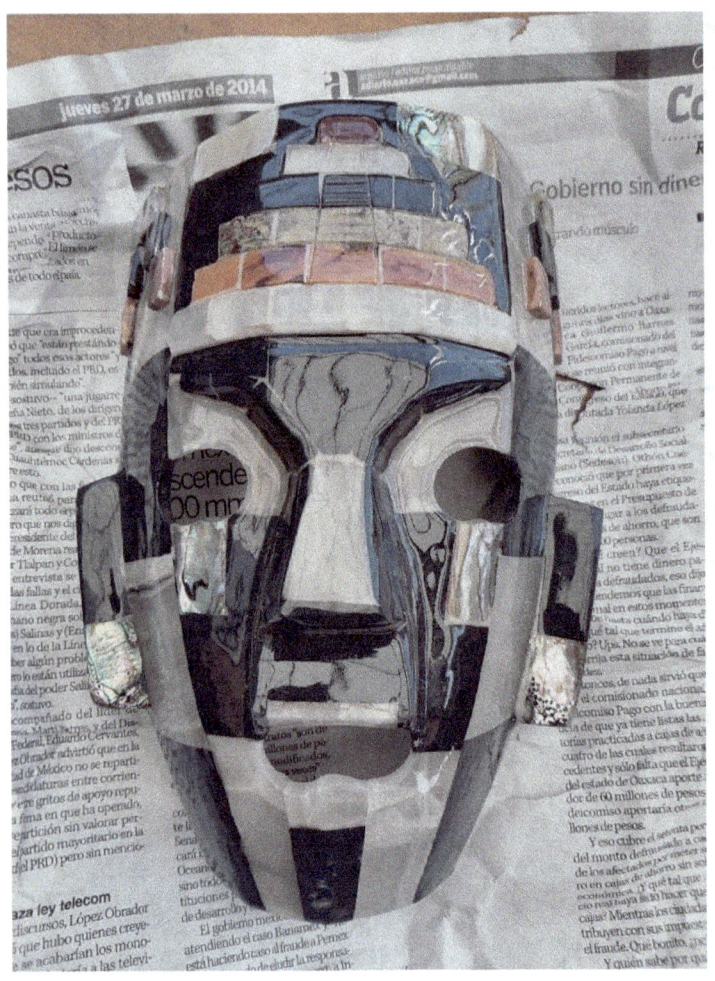

A mask I bought man made by Danny Di Paa depicting their dark ancient ancestors made of obsidian, Jade, and Quartz crystals

Thought I would have 4 more exciting months with the Centruroides nigrimanuses here in Oaxaca City, Mexico, I must return soon.

Peace and Love from the Bird Mound

www.ingramcontent.com/pod-product-compliance
Lightning Source LLC
LaVergne TN
LVHW022001060526
838201LV00048B/1653